THE NEW MOM'S GUIDE TO

Living on Baby Time

Susan Besze Wallace
with Monica Reed, MD

Revell

a division of Baker Publishing Group
Grand Rapids, Michigan

© 2009 by MOPS International

Published by Revell
a division of Baker Publishing Group
P.O. Box 6287, Grand Rapids, MI 49516-6287
www.revellbooks.com

Printed in the United States of America

Library of Congress Cataloging-in-Publication Data
Wallace, Susan Besze, 1969–
    The new mom's guide to living on baby time / Susan Besze Wallace
  with Monica Reed, M.D.
        p.   cm. — (The new mom's guides ; bk. 2)
    ISBN 978-0-8007-3299-8 (pbk.)
    1. Mothers. 2. Mother and infant. 3. Infants—Care. I. Reed, Monica.
  II. Title.
  HQ759.W314 2009
  649.122—dc22   2008041106

The information provided herein should not be construed as prescribed health-care advice or instruction. The information is provided with the understanding that the publisher does not enter into a health-care practitioner/patient relationship with its readers. Readers who rely on information in this publication to replace the advice of health-care professionals, or who fail to consult with health-care professionals, assume all risks of such conduct.

Published in association with the literary agency of Alive Communications, Inc., 7680 Goddard Street, Suite 200, Colorado Springs, CO 80920.

THE NEW MOM'S GUIDE TO

Living on
Baby Time

Introduction

My New Center

Contents

Contents

I was standing at the kitchen counter, poised to attack the stacks of mail and bills and newspapers and dirty dishtowels surrounding me, and I heard it—my new baby's cry.

No. Not yet. Not again. I haven't gotten anything done. I haven't even showered. The books said he should nap about two hours. I tried to will him back to sleep. I even muttered a prayer under my breath. *Pleeeease, not yet. I need to do* my *stuff.*

He wailed again.

I unclenched my fists and my eyes and made my way to my baby's room.

I'd spent my son's young life trying to deal with him—nourish him, situate him—so I could get back to *my* stuff. I thought that was a mom's routine. But for some reason, on this day, a lightbulb went on, as I felt defeated by the number of things on my to-do list. A voice inside said, *He isn't a thing.* He is *the* thing, my "stuff," my new center. And whatever else I thought was so important to do, that should move to the sidelines for now.

It was a beautiful, pivotal, helpful moment for me as a new mom who thrived, and still thrives, on being productive. Of course that didn't help me write overdue thank-you notes, descudge my floor, or read something more invigorating than the ibuprofen bottle. You get the picture. You are probably living it.

Before kids, you controlled most things—when you ate, when you showered, how long you took to dry your hair, and whether you called in sick to work. Now a baby's rhythms of eating, needing to be held, playing, and sleeping dictate the use of your days—and your nights. You might not have expected motherhood to feel so all-encompassing, so stifling at moments. Even when motherhood feels wonderful, it's overwhelming.

"This too shall pass," my mom always likes to say. But we can *enjoy* the passage of these baby days, not just survive them. And we should. Our children absorb our attitudes—and our stress—from the get-go. Breathe deeply and get ready to take a look inside your mothering so far—what you do and how you feel about it. You always have enough time to be inspired by a new idea for making the most of this very unique season of life.

What's Normal

Adjusting Your Expectations

Every morning when I lifted a little body out of a crib, big blue eyes looking to me for direction and nourishment, I felt a stabbing sense of being alone. That was true with my first child, when the only other sound around was the tinkling of a dog collar. It was true with my second, as I started juggling conversations with a preschooler while caring for the baby. And it was true with my third, when there were two other kids romping or eating breakfast while I locked eyes with the baby for the first time that day. I still felt alone.

It wasn't a scary alone, like walking through a haunted house (though cobwebs were increasingly easy to find!). It was more of a heaviness, knowing

I was the one who would choose everything that would touch my child's life that day, and most days. I would decide what he would eat and wear and whom he would see. I would choose where he would sleep and what he would hear. With each baby it was at once exciting and overwhelming. The days rolled forward, and the decisions collected like a snowball rolling downhill. Early on I didn't take many opportunities to stop and see what shape the snowball was taking or to pick the twigs out or just to stop rolling once in a while.

The question that pummeled me day after day after day was this: Was I doing it *right*? Millions of women were doing the same thing, but how did *they* do it? Did they dress baby *before* breakfast? Give a bath in the morning or at night? Had they started baby sign language at this age? Did they sleep when the baby did, as the books insisted? Maybe they were already out losing baby bulge

"You hear it and you hear it: 'Cherish those moments.' But that is truly incredible advice when I look back. I wrote down my son's firsts—when that tooth came in, his first word—but they are just on two sheets of paper in the front of a baby book—a baby book that isn't put together. He's five! I was too busy to cherish the moments. I think you have to make a conscious decision to focus on those important moments, even if you have to let some things go. Because time will go. I had a friend in elementary school, and all I remember about her house is that her mom was cleaning every single time I was there. I don't want to be that mom."

Vanessa

by pushing the jogger stroller. Maybe they had nannies and were still in the sack at 9 a.m.

Are you wondering if you're missing something that will make life easier, more enjoyable, and less exhausting? My experience to date says you will always wonder. You should indeed take stock of your routine and strive to do things well, but new moms tend to get whiplash trying to keep up with the volley of advice on raising baby coming their way.

Slow down. Sit down.

For a moment let go of the how-to books, the clock, the thoughts about what other moms are doing. Look squarely at the unique little life that is blessing you. Love that baby. Your days—and all those decisions—will fall into place just fine. You have time to work on the details, but that moment you just gazed at your baby—that particular moment—is gone forever. You've just been told what millions of moms find out the hard way.

So how do you actually let go or even just loosen up on expectations? First, give yourself time. There's a lot of change happening at once, and it is indeed overwhelming. It's taken a long time to become the person you are, and you will not likely break old habits overnight. For example, if you are a fastidious housekeeper—some may even call you a neat freak—the idea of going to bed with a sink full of dishes might be inconceivable. Eventually, you will have to decide if twenty more minutes of sleep—now—is more important to you than a clean kitchen.

Writing thank-you notes was a tough one for me. I would keep going until my handwriting deteriorated, and I actually remember once falling asleep while writing a note to a friend who'd sent a baby gift. But it's how I was raised. You write them, and you do it quickly. But writing a thank-you note to me is the last thing I want a new mom to be doing in her "free" time. Unless it truly makes her feel good. For the record, by my third son's premature birth, I was still writing thank-yous, but it took me months—and I never put them before visiting him in the hospital or getting sleep.

In addition to being easier on yourself, ask if there's an old way of doing things that isn't jibing with your new way of life with a newborn. Making dinner comes to mind. Countless times I'd start a meal only to have the baby need to eat or have that late afternoon period of fussiness. I would feel like a failure for not being able to make a simple meal. I'm not suggesting you "let go" of the expectation that you'll eat dinner. You need to eat and eat healthy. Just adjust your way of thinking. Cereal or PB&J for dinner is OK sometimes. So is making something easy earlier in the day—or in the week—and having it ready to pop in the oven. The Crock-Pot quickly became my greatest dinner ally.

Getting out of the house will also never be the same. It takes longer, and you will likely be late getting places sometimes. You can beat yourself up or accept the change and look for new strategies for timing your departure better.

Talking to other moms helps. Hearing that you share the same struggles may help you adjust your way of thinking. For me, putting things on paper helps me actually see what it is I'm trying to do. Write down exactly what has to get done, and then write down what else you'd do if you could. Learn to keep your lists manageable and realistic. I realized at one point my lists were paralyzing me because they had no priorities. Painting a room and getting milk at the store were on the same notepad. My friend Michelle told me that one time she had her infant daughter in a car seat, ready to head out, when she picked up her list and took stock.

"I sat right back down and unbuckled the baby. Nothing really had to be done that moment," she said. "I realized I was keeping myself busy because I was used to working with lots of goals and deadlines. That was my biggest adjustment, adjusting my ideas on what I thought was really urgent."

Living on Baby Time
My Rattled Daze

1. What did I expect life to be like when I first brought my baby home? How does reality compare to that expectation?

2. How have I adjusted my expectations of what I can accomplish in one day?

3. How do I cope with having to put some of my plans and goals on hold?

Spin Cycle

Taking Life One Load at a Time

It is quite normal for a new mom to feel like a hamster on a wheel. The twenty-four-hour eating and sleeping cycle of a newborn means the days run together, the days and nights certainly run together, and your pre-baby idea of what a mom-day looks like might have run away altogether. This is a short-lived yet intense period of time. By the time you finish one feeding and maybe feed yourself, it's about time to feed the baby again. Remember, this is normal and temporary.

Many women find that faithfully practicing an eat-activity-sleep pattern for their babies creates a pleasing blueprint for their days. Some found a version of this method in Tracey Hogg's *The Baby Whisperer*, while others, like me, learned it from friends and family. Having a suggested framework for your days helps you know what to expect and know what to do and when.

Here's the drill. Baby eats. Baby has awake time or playtime, no longer than fifteen minutes early on, lengthening naturally as baby gets older and is more aware of his surroundings. Then baby is put to bed—drowsy but awake. Making sure your baby goes through each of these phases with each feeding seems to lead naturally into longer naps and that coveted through-the-night sleep for you both. Resisting the urge to feed your child until he goes to sleep is crucial in helping your baby learn to soothe himself. And it's tough for immature digestive systems to be laid down with air bubbles stuck inside, so if a baby falls asleep eating, he may not sleep long. You might diagnose your baby as a finicky sleeper, when actually he's uncomfortable from the very thing that gave him comfort—or he fell asleep before getting a full feeding. By my third son, I was a believer that usually sticking to

"I always thought baby days would be just sheer fun. I'd stopped working and thought I'd have all this time on my hands. To come from a job where you hand in reports and attend meetings and see things actually advance on a daily basis, mommy stuff can blow your mind in its sameness. They were fun days, but they were a little numbing sometimes."

Ann

this pattern, even waking him up gently for a few minutes if he fell asleep during a feeding, was best for creating good eating and sleeping habits. That said, being flexible and learning your own baby's patterns are essential.

I understand how easy it is to feed or hold or rock a baby to sleep. I did it for a while. The consequences seem affordable on a day-to-day basis. And it feels good. It doesn't feel good, however, when you are still doing it every nap and every night when the child is two. Investing in good sleep habits will pay huge dividends for you and your kids as they grow up.

Once the baby has a rhythm—not an unyielding schedule but a rhythm—you can take stock of your own patterns each day.

Going from a work environment to being home with a baby can be a shock to the system. I was used to daily feedback. Now no one was handing out evaluations. I was used to adult interaction and decisions that would eventually reach millions of people. Now I was talking baby nonsense and was hyperfocused on one person's bowel movements.

When I was working, I planned things, created things, finished things. I didn't realize how much of a productivity junkie I was until I had a baby and couldn't get my fix.

On arrival, babies do demand, and deserve, all of you. Give it to them. And then rest. And then give them more. And then rest. You have permission to lay many of life's details aside. You are tired. And while it might give you a temporary rush of adrenalin to keep up with your old self, your new self needs time to absorb life's changes. If there is a day—or many days—that the only accomplishment you can list is taking care of the baby and maybe unloading the dishwasher, that is just fine. You will catch up on the other things soon enough. This is life with an infant.

You're thinking, *But wait, they sleep so much! I can do all sorts of things.* Sure, some days. But it's

"I think the part of
motherhood
that still makes me crazy is never
seeing anything 'done,' except
maybe dinner, but even that has
to be done again the next day.
The cycle is so mundane, the
gratification so delayed. The
person who weathers the first six
months of motherhood well is
the person who can walk away
from things with perspective,
the person who can say, 'Oh
well, there goes another
two hours.' No one else on
the planet will see the sense of
urgency you do about things.
Moms are just so anxious to
complete things."

Lisa

important not to set yourself up for frustration or failure.

Long before kids, I reported, from a Coast Guard boat, on a story about shark endangerment. I didn't know that's where I was headed that day, so my pearls and slacks made quite a statement. Once we were out in the Gulf of Mexico, a storm blew in. The rocking and rolling of the waves threw me everywhere. I locked my knees in self-defense and tried to see through the spitting rain. I fell down more than once. And then I threw up.

The sailor who handed me a barf bag down below deck told me gently: "Your knees. You have to bend your knees so you can be ready for anything."

So it goes with daily mothering. Storms *will* arise. Rigidity can lead to a big mess. Forethought is huge. And pearls and slacks are usually not the best choice.

My sister decided to make her own birth announcements for her first child. She had them 75

"All I wanted to do was sit and stare at him all day. I'm glad for that. I watched him sleep. I watched the twinkle in his eye develop. My world was consumed by that."

Tristan's mom

percent done before he was born. We sat together one day in a sea of blue plaid scraps, happy as can be until my new nephew woke and fussed and fussed. My sister's frustration grew as he cried louder. I glued faster, he kept crying, and she kept working until we were finished. Years later we had a good laugh remembering how intense we were about something so unnecessary. Our knees were most certainly not bent.

We are a multitasking generation, and we have to be. When it's time to get three children out the door for school, you need the skills that allow you to hold cupcakes in one arm, baby in another, keys between your teeth, and the door with your foot while pleasantly urging your preschooler to leave Elmo at home and your kindergartener to flush the toilet. That was my yesterday. And I'm darn proud of it, since for a long time I could hardly feed the baby and talk on the phone at the same time. But I think sometimes we should stop layering tasks

Daylight

Tips for Your Time and Spirit

❀ Once your baby hits about a month old, try to begin and end your days at generally the same time. The predictability will be great for baby, and heartening for you too. Grabbing that twenty extra minutes of sleep if you can seems like a good idea, but not if it's going to make you feel behind the rest of the day.

❀ Shower—quickly if you have to. It's fine to do it while baby is awake—at 3 a.m. if that's what works. But shower! Having a fresh start at some point in the day makes a difference.

❀ Make a list to sort out the things whirling about in your head, but don't be glued to it or defeated by it. Try two sections: what must be done and what could be done. It might feel silly at first, but go ahead and write things like "Sing to my daughter" or "Tell my husband I love him" to help with prioritizing.

❀ Get out of the house. Maybe it's just to sweep your porch or walk to the mailbox. Sunshine and fresh air will boost your mood and remind you of life beyond your walls. If the weather is crummy, find a change of scenery in your own home. Just feeding the baby in a different room can be a pleasant change.

❀ Get a newspaper. Read something, however short, that has to do with current events, not about being a mom. Consider joining or starting a book club. The mental stimulation, grown-up discussion, and satisfaction of finishing something are gratifying.

❀ Consider ways to be productive and focused at the same time. For example, plan a day to make several dinners ahead of time and freeze them. Narrate what you're doing to your baby while he swings nearby. When a day is rocky, you'll have a good frozen meal that will help preserve a little sanity and energy at dinnertime.

so much. My mom never talked on a cell phone while she drove. She didn't even drive until after she had had three children.

Children need on-their-level eye contact. That's impossible if you are too busy to bend down. The choices you make right now for you and your baby are setting a tone for your household. You can choose between a tone that's harried and uptight or one that is flexible and peaceful. Set the right priorities during these days, and it will pay off as your children grow up.

Living on Baby Time
My Rattled Daze

1. How's my rhythm? What would I like to tweak about my child's routine, and where might I seek advice?

2. What's been the toughest adjustment to motherhood for me so far?

3. How would I rate myself as a multitasker? What could help me focus more fully on my baby?

Offbeat

Doing What Works
for Your Family

I still remember the look on my friend's grinning face as I sat in mommy confession with her. Today's sin: taking a shower while my new baby sat a foot away in his bouncy seat—*awake*. I was rationalizing all over the place: *He didn't seem to be too lonely; I looked out at him seven times; I was really gnarly; I usually wait until he's sleeping.*

She laughed at me and claimed my experiment was a mainstay of motherhood. "Don't you dare waste baby's nap on taking a shower!" she said. And then quite seriously she looked me in the eye and added, "Do what works for you."

Do what works for you. What anguish could be prevented if moms heard and truly believed that was okay. There is no other mom-baby combination in the universe that is you. While books give you tips, insights, and strategies, they are best used with your own mother's gut, as you create a safe, happy, and healthy place for your child to grow up. Don't think certain strategies are "wrong" until you've run them through a network of other loving, noncompetitive moms. You might already be on the right track and just don't trust yourself.

My friend Vanessa and I had our first sons six months apart. She planned out her time—even creating note cards out of *The Baby Whisperer* on creating a pattern for her new days as a mom. I remember my shock the first time I heard that Vanessa put her son down for the night at 10 p.m. She and her husband went to bed about 1 a.m. Her husband worked from home, so the whole family slept in till about 10 o'clock in the morning.

"It was different, but it worked great for us," she said. "It wasn't until talking to other people that I

A Day in My Life
Putting Life in My Daze

With a newborn, it seems time is not your own. And sometimes when an unexpected pocket of peace does present itself, it can be gone before you decide what to do with it. Keep these following ideas handy to consider, and you'll probably have more and more opportunity for them as your baby grows older each week.

- **A new activity for baby**: Sing a new song, walk a different path, tell her a story about her extended family.

- **A comforting activity for me**: Call a good friend, read a new novel, take a bubble bath, record my journey in a journal.

- **An enhancing activity for my home**: Clean out a drawer, plant flowers while baby enjoys fresh air, frame or file new pictures of the baby.

- **A supportive activity for my husband**: Write a love note to reconnect, rent a movie to "share" during feeding shifts, make his favorite dessert.

- **A visionary activity for my community**: Join a local MOPS (Mothers of Preschoolers) group (www.MOPS. org), donate outgrown clothes or new baby supplies to a shelter for women and children, strike up a conversation with an elderly neighbor.

realized no one else was doing what we were. You learn to stand your ground when others express their opinions. I'm sure some people thought I was weird."

I admit I was one of those people. It was hard to have a morning date to the park with Vanessa since her morning was my noon! But I admired the way her family functioned—and her confidence in her choices. She'll tell you she compared herself with other moms and wondered like the rest of us if she was doing the right thing. But when she chose a path, she didn't make excuses for it.

Sometimes the transition home with a baby feels both exciting and intimidating, like a blank canvas. There can be pressure in wanting to "draw" the perfect days, even though you are tired and just getting used to all your new responsibilities. I think it can be helpful if a new mom doesn't overscrutinize each day, but looks at her hopes and goals over time, a week perhaps. Maybe Tuesday was a day of blowout diapers and a four-feeding night, but Thursday was a trip to the mall and the chance to call your mom. Don't score each day. Rather give yourself grace; consider yourself a student learning over a very challenging school year.

Several teacher friends shared with me how they brought their training to bear and started writing a "lesson plan" for their days as new moms. It wasn't a strict, teach-your-newborn-his-colors lesson plan, but more of a personal strategy for getting through the day and getting a few things done. Even a list maker like me hadn't thought of trying to put into words the overall mission for my days—especially with the busyness of a new baby. If I had done this, it might have cleared the fog a little.

"It held me accountable when I felt like no one was holding me accountable," one teacher friend, Erika, told me.

"All the books said you should get up before your child to get that head start. I was never good at that, but I still needed a way to get centered each day. I would get up and feed the baby and put her back in her crib with the mobile on. I got ready pretty quickly, but as I got ready, I lit a candle each day.

"I would say, 'God, give me the strength to do what you want me to do today.' It just gave me a little inner peace, a quiet ahhh moment. I thought if *I* needed that to get started, my daughter did too. So we both got that time. My kids still get that time as I get ready. The candle was just a great trick for me."

You'll likely discover plenty of tricks in the coming years, such as peaceful grocery shopping at 10 p.m., when your husband is home to babysit; throwing pureed vegetables into brownies for the nutritional value; or hiding dryer sheets under your seat to get rid of that smell in your car. Enjoy the journey of discovery, and remember, finding your family's groove takes a while. What works with one baby might not work with the next. What works one *week* might not work the next. My hope is that you are able, in the weary excitement of this precious time, to see that while you don't control your time as you used to, you do have options and the freedom to try out those options.

Living on Baby Time
My Rattled Daze

1. What works for me? Do I like a scheduled day or an unscheduled day?

2. What's one thing I can do daily to help me feel some sort of routine exists in my life right now?

3. How have I tailored my routine to my family's needs?

Staying
Flexible

What Rattles Your Rhythm

Perhaps it is no accident that during the days I was writing this chapter, my two-and-a-half-year-old threw up on me. Two days later I walked away from the computer to find my five-and-a-half-year-old tossing his cookies too. There was a time that this would have thrown my entire week into a tizzy of doctor calls and hourly husband updates and major anxiety. Barfing babies scared me.

Over time I've become much less tightly wound about things I can't control. It can be a beautiful benefit of motherhood, this mellowing out, especially since the days *without* craziness or crisis can sometimes feel like the abnormal ones. At this moment I have a jumbo bottle of window cleaner under my sink, with a table knife lodged in it. I'm pretty sure I know which kid did it and when—can't imagine why—but I've decided not to make it a big deal. After spending five minutes a day trying to get the knife out, ensuring my fingers would smell like ammonia for a month, I just had to laugh and move on. There it sits under the sink.

A few weeks ago my toddler son snuck in the kitchen and tried earnestly to make hot chocolate all by himself. I really battle with the nonstop goo in my house these days and how it makes me feel unkempt as a woman and as a housekeeper. The gritty brown sludge I saw coating him and my kitchen could have sent me over the edge. Instead it sent me to the camera to record a moment in time—in his time—that was actually quite beautiful.

I can imagine your eyes rolling. But trust me, it took a while for this control freak to get to this place. And I'm not always there.

Poet Maya Angelou says you can tell a lot about a person by how he or she handles lost luggage, a rainy day, and tangled Christmas tree lights. Curse words and foot stomping come to mind? Those won't help you much as a mom. Good baggage tags, an umbrella kept where you need it, and a sense of humor will get you much farther—in a word, *preparation*. Here are some things known to throw moms into a frenzy, and some ideas on persevering through them.

Doctor Visits and Immunizations

A visit to the pediatrician was often a high point in my weeks as a new mom. Not only did it force me out, but I found out how much weight my baby had gained. Each new ounce felt like a validation of all I was giving and going through at home. But I struggled with finding the right time for each visit. When you are feeding a baby around the clock, it's pretty hard to time an appointment so it doesn't coincide with a feeding during the trip to or from or actually in the doctor's office. Don't try too hard. Doctors see plenty of fussy babies and moms who nurse while they wait.

Just the stimulation of the visit can make baby cry, and immunizations can make you both want to cry. Seeing your baby poked by a needle may be harder on you than on the baby. When doctors' appointments came in the morning, I always planned to do something for myself—at home— in the afternoon. The shots seemed to bring on a deep afternoon nap for the baby, which I was willing to let go a little longer knowing what he'd been through.

Shots can also result in fussiness and a low-grade fever in the days to come, so I tried not to plan outings during those days—and I always had infant Tylenol on hand.

If doctor's appointments seem challenging to you, time them near your husband's lunch hour so he can go along, or ask Grandma to accompany you for support. Many years after my first baby's doctor's visits, I still write down the issues or questions I want to cover with the doctor. I simply can't remember them all on my own while dealing with kids in an exam room.

Growth Spurts

Growth spurts are otherwise known as confidence thieves. Baby gets fussy, seems to eat nonstop, or starts waking at night just when you thought the stretches of sleep were getting longer. You wonder about your milk production. You question your choice of formula. Your husband questions you. Your frustration simmers. You thought you had this down.

Stay the course! Growth spurts can happen at any time, but watch for them at about seven to ten days old, two to three weeks, four to six weeks, three months, four months, six months, and nine months old. They can last a couple of days or up to a week.

Respond to your baby's signals. If he's hungry, feed him. Nursing moms will see their milk production catch up with baby's demands in a day or so. Keep drinking lots of water. For formula babies, the American Academy of Pediatrics recommends that babies take in about two and one-half ounces of formula a day for every pound of body weight. Do your math and make sure you are keeping pace. Also consider that if your baby is sleeping longer at night, he may need more milk during the day. If your child is older than four months, he may be showing signs of being ready for cereal. Discuss this with your doctor.

How do you know that this burst of certainty-busting was really growth? Look for your child to sleep a little harder or longer for a couple of days and for your breasts and baby's diapers to feel fuller. Watch for this pattern to repeat itself and don't get discouraged. Your intuition is being honed with each growth spurt you identify. One day you'll see the signs clearly in your growing toddler.

Illness

There is nothing harder than trying to parent when you long to jump in bed and wallow in the misery of a cold. Your head is pounding, your eyes are watering, and your throat is scratchy. Anyone else would pick up the phone and take a sick day. Moms rarely get one.

It's just as draining emotionally as physically to be a sick mom. You experience an odd combination of feeling trapped, guilty, and resentful. Those feelings, while valid, aren't going to help you get better. If you are in need of help, you must find it. Ask your husband to stay home. If you don't tell him, he doesn't know how clogged your head is or how bad that tooth hurts.

If you do have to muddle through on your own, be careful about the medicine you take for relief, especially making sure it's safe if you are nursing. You don't want a drug making you too fuzzy to function. Let go of the housework for a while, and know that it's okay to curl up with a blanket on the floor as your baby plays in a safe, contained area.

Don't spread germs by going to your playgroups or other commitments. Calling in reinforcements to help you is tricky since you don't want to expose anyone else to your illness. But if your baby is well, consider asking a friend to take her for a walk. Other moms would probably be happy to get you a few groceries, even if they choose to leave them on your porch. Wouldn't you do the same? Creating that go-to network will never happen if someone doesn't make the first move. Having it in place is a beautiful thing.

My friend Sara is among those tough-as-nails women who are sick nearly their entire pregnancies. Trying to parent a child, while growing a child, while throwing up every day, gave her a new perspective on trying to do it all. "Your children will not remember that you pawned them off for a few days," she says. "You cannot be afraid to take the help when you need it. That's exactly what you'd tell a friend, so you have to listen to yourself."

Preventing illness takes on new meaning when your job is 24-7. Stay healthy by getting all the sleep you can and taking a multivitamin. And here's a plug for hand washing: there is no better way to keep your kids or yourself from getting sick. It's not the soap you use; it's how long you wash. Twenty seconds at the sink can help keep colds as well as serious respiratory illnesses and diarrhea at bay.

Sleep Struggles

Perhaps nothing requires more patience and flexibility from a mom than her child's sleep habits.

Volumes have been written on how to cultivate healthy nap and bedtime practices, and there is much sound advice to be had. I'd be remiss if I didn't mention the family-changing potential of books like *The Baby Whisperer*; *Sleep Solutions for Your Baby, Toddler, and Preschooler*; and *Healthy Sleep Habits, Happy Child*. Thank goodness these resources exist. Use them; highlight them; put them to the test. However, *your* approach to sleep is a chapter only *you* can write. It needs to include humor, flexibility, realistic expectations, and the acknowledgment that every child is different and no phase is forever.

I have a few thoughts on riding out the waves of sleep inconsistencies. Make sure you are parenting a person, not a schedule. As this book began, I recounted how I fought against my son's sleep instead of rolling with it. Someone reminded me along the way that we adults don't just fall asleep with the flick of a switch at someone else's discretion. Far from it. Our minds spin, our stomachs rumble, or the noises of the night keep us from settling down. Remembering this helped—and still helps—when I get frustrated with a non-napper or early riser. It also helps me to know that sleep isn't something to fool around with. It's a sound place to invest your parental energy and creativity. Being consistent—again not rigid—with naps and bedtimes produces a good sleeper, which in turn means a healthier child who learns better and is generally in a better mood.

It still amazes me that overtired children fight sleep. It goes against conventional wisdom, doesn't it? *I'll keep him up longer so he'll plunge into a three-hour nap. I'll let him stay up Friday night so he'll sleep in Saturday morning.* It doesn't work that way. If you miss a baby or child's drowsy window and he gets too tired, falling asleep could involve some serious fussing, and you may have unwittingly set the stage for a shorter nap.

I had a few other sleep "awakenings" too. My oldest stopped settling well into an afternoon nap at about six months old. I struggled and struggled and finally it dawned on me—he needed lunch. Sound obvious? I was a first-time mom, a first-time feeder of jar foods. I'd started with breakfast and then added dinner, as my pediatrician suggested. I just never thought much about lunch. But extra calories made an instant difference. When he got older, a similar wakefulness happened again at naptime. I started taking him out, playing a little while, and then trying again. Seems he wasn't tired anymore at the naptime I'd established. So I had to go with his flow—his own drowsy times. A half-hour change solved the problem. It was a great lesson for me.

Remember to go with your baby's flow when one day it comes time for her to drop a nap. It will rearrange your schedule, but your schedule is not effective unless it suits your child. This

How Much Sleep Do They Need?

This guide is a compilation of what pediatricians and parenting experts advise for sleep. Don't fret if your child is off a bit, but straying too far from these sleep amounts could create a foundation for fussiness and growth challenges. Consult your pediatrician if your child's wakefulness is a concern.

Age	Number of Naps	Total Sleep Hours
1 week	through the day	16.5
1 month	3	15.5
3 months	3	15
6 months	2	14.25
9 months	2	14
12 months	2	13.75
18 months	1	13.5
2 years	1	13
3 years	1	12
4 years	0	11–12
5 years	0	11
10 years	0	9.75
adolescent	0	9.25*

*they usually get about 7.5 hours due to biological rhythms and early school start times

makes sense, and though it's good to read about the proper care of baby, often we must just go with our common sense.

Teething

It's a joke in our house with any low-grade fever or crankiness to blame it on teething. I think my husband even asked *me* once: "New teeth coming in?" Whether or not that's the source of the angst, it's nice to blame it on something. Teething usually begins between four and nine months, with at least a first tooth forming a gum bump and then popping through by the time baby turns one. That said, I've seen a child get that first chomper at four months, and another pop one at thirteen and a half months. First to show up is usually the bottom front pair of incisors, but two of my sons got their top ones first—very beaveresque!

Children handle teething differently. My nephew wore drool-drenched clothes for several months. I hardly saw spit when my boys were teething. In time the range of teething symptoms gets easier to spot and pull together in your mind as you assess what's going on with your baby. Those symptoms include irritability, drooling, disturbed sleep, an extra-saliva cough without a cold or flu, and gnawing on anything they can hold. Eating irregularities—like pursing lips to keep the spoon out—can also point to a mouth in pain.

Not all doctors agree that diarrhea and a low-grade fever are linked to teething, but I'd swear they are. When those symptoms last more than a couple days you should consult your pediatrician. When you consider all that kids are putting in their mouths, as well as the is-there-a-tooth-in-there checks you may be doing, the fever could be a sign of illness. It's imperative to keep yours and baby's hands clean to keep germs from adding illness to teething woes.

If your child is having a rough teething day, consider tanking your plans for the day. It's not convenient, but when's the last time *you* tried to put on a smile and have a normal day with a toothache? Teething rings can be helpful, although that was the one thing my kids *wouldn't* chew on. The numbing gels just annoyed them. Ibuprofen or acetaminophen, given with a doctor's approval, was the only thing that gave my kids relief.

Introducing a Bottle

If you ask a number of nursing moms if, when, and how you should introduce a bottle, you'll get no consensus. Some women wait just a few weeks after birth to introduce a bottle, but their babies refuse to take it. Others wait a few months, and their kids seem not to have any confusion about going back and forth. If you want baby and bottle to be friends, and they're not, it can be very troubling.

On the rare occasions we would leave our oldest son, Zach, with a babysitter for an evening, we'd come home to find he had taken perhaps an ounce from a bottle. I'd crumple in guilt. Our youngest, A.J., went happily between a bottle and me until pneumonia put him in the hospital. Then I was all too happy to nurse him exclusively because it seemed to be the one thing I could do to comfort him. He never took a bottle again. I was disappointed and kept trying, but there wasn't any guilt this time because I realized that I could try a cup at any time and he wasn't going to starve. Dozens of women I know have experienced the joy of nursing with the baggage of not ever being able to leave baby and a bottle behind successfully. Try giving your baby a cup, and try not to worry. When baby begins eating solids, his tummy will fill up, and you can spend time away from him knowing he will be satisfied. If you are at ease about this, your husband or caregiver will be too. Don't use your baby's refusal to take a bottle as an excuse not to take breaks from home and baby. Nursing loses much of its benefit if you get resentful.

Trusting Your Instincts

Sometimes newer moms feel inferior to those with more children and more experience, and they're tempted to ditch their own instincts. I was especially prone to this on trips and around relatives. For example, say you are at the park with some new friends. You feel your child is nearing naptime, but so far she's doing well, and you don't want to seem like a sleep Nazi, so you stick around. The other mothers don't seem concerned about naptime and *they must know what they are doing, right?* Twenty minutes later, your baby erupts into wails of overstimulation, and your park departure and drive home are miserable.

Enough uncontrollable things rattle your rhythm as a mom without you doing it to yourself, just because you want to fit in or put on a good face. You are the only one who is mom to your child. No one else will protect his naps, anticipate his meals, or care about the condition of his rear end quite like you. When you embrace this fact, you become not just your child's biological beginning but his advocate.

On the flip side is the mom who can't admit she's learning and is so staunch in her ideas and paralyzed by her schedule that she drives others away. Make no mistake, we are all learning, all the time.

A word on the mom with three kids or more, the one you see deftly steering a double stroller and maybe holding hands with another child. You wonder, *How in the world would I do three when I can barely do one?* Please don't get ahead of yourself. Yes, one seems easy by comparison when you have two or three or four children. But there's not a mom in the world who hasn't felt her hands completely full

Picture This

The adrenalin was pumping.

Not only had I been a mom for just thirteen days, but I was with my parents—first-time, adoring grandparents—and we were on a mission to get Zach's first picture. Sort of the Bermuda Triangle of common sense.

We arrived at Kiddie Kandids and put our names on a list. I had enough experience in my thirteen days to know I needed to feed Zach while I could. My dad wandered through babyland, and Mom accompanied me to the lounge. Zach nursed as we heard muffled names being called over the store's intercom.

I started to change the baby when my dad banged on the door, telling us it was our turn. At that very moment, Zach's exposed penis shot pee through the air with such force that it showered both his head and the wall behind him. The outfit was spared, barely.

We made it to the cameras, at which point I brought out the little hat that went with the outfit that was drowning him, though the tag told me it should fit. The hat was too big too, but I was so insistent he wear it, that we paper clipped it together in the back.

Well, we survived and got some great pictures to boot. My sweet boy was so exhausted that he conked out on the living room couch. My dog curled up next to him in virtually the same position for her own nap. Now *that* was a good picture.

I've been through the picture-taking ordeal many times since—minus the projectile pee. Often I get anxious and start to sweat, but the experience is always a reminder of our limits as moms.

Here are some tips for enjoying the experience.

- If your photographer can't handle the rhythms of children with patience and compassion, find another one.

- Try for the morning's first appointment or walk-in opportunity.

- Take a helper. Having another set of hands is great, especially when multiple kids are involved in the photo.

- Beware of feeding your child seconds before you manhandle her, if you want clothes to stay clean. Get her to produce a good burp.

- Forget overalls. While darling on a hanger, they bunch up and gap in weird places on children who can't stand.

- Your attitude is everything, and children sense your unease. Have fun with it. You don't want a picture that screams "My mom made me do this."

- Chop the props. A rocker or wagon is nice, but be wary of using so many add-ins that your child is lost in the shuffle. What seems like a good idea in the studio can later appear to be busy, hokey pictures. You can't go wrong with a sweet face—smiling or not—and a white background.

- Check your expectations at the door. My first attempt at having two kids photographed together resulted in a picture of Zach holding a sleeping newborn Luke. He simply couldn't stay awake. Oh well, it was real life.

- If you are photographing just one of your children and your other children are young, make sure they have something to do during the process or something to look forward to when it's over. With the photographer's permission, enlist their help in keeping the subject entertained and smiling. Sometimes they're best at it!

- Be willing to call it a day if your child is howling and you feel yourself starting to lose your patience. No picture is worth stressing out either of you.

- Consider waiting to order photos. Choose to come back rather than make a selection with a crying infant needing you. Many women have wished they had stepped back before ordering more pictures than they needed or choosing one that later didn't seem to capture the child they know.

with her first child. She is lying if she says otherwise, or she has a highly selective memory.

Living on Baby Time
My Rattled Daze

1. What rattles me the most? How could I change my reaction to that?

2. How can I listen to the advice of other moms without thinking I have to follow their pattern completely? What would help me sift through it all and decide what is right for my baby and me?

3. How can I involve my husband in decisions I must make about baby's sleep, seeking a doctor's advice, and other choices I must make daily?

5

Tears
and Fears

Coping with Crying

Sometimes the unique direction our days take is not of our choosing. Colic throws many families for a loop. This phenomenon of hours-long crying usually hits your baby suddenly and in the evening. The National Institutes of Health says about 20 percent of babies cry enough to meet the definition of colic, which begins most often when baby is three weeks old and usually lifts by twelve weeks.

Like many moms whose babies have colic, my friend Liz's "lesson plan" for her day was simply survival. She'd put on headphones each night and hold a screaming infant, something she had to do for both her children.

"She would start crying at 5 p.m. and go till about 9:30. Of course Brian was home then, so that was all he saw of her. You feel like you have to fix it, to do the right thing. The noise of your baby's cry affects you like nothing else. You feel so helpless. But accepting that, that you are sort of helpless, was a huge turning point in my getting through it."

Liz

"Someone gave me the analogy of thinking what it would be like to go to a foreign country where you didn't speak the language and couldn't communicate with a soul. That's your miserable baby," Liz said. "It helped me, seeing it like that. It allowed me not to get angry at my kids but to just feel sad for them. I felt like I was the only one dealing with it, and it felt like an eternity."

Motherhood tests us all, but colic is like a twelve-week bar exam—beyond intense. The parent of a colicky baby knows a different depth of uncertainty and vulnerability.

Hang in there. Your child needs you.

The more your baby cries, the more you want to be the one to soothe, the one to provide the breakthrough. Please, take a break. Take a walk. Even just an hour away can refuel you. Your baby needs *you*, not the hollow-eyed, crazy lady you will become if you don't step away once in a while. Friends and neighbors want to help. Let them.

Share your struggles verbally too. It's normal to feel angry or down. Be willing to vent.

When your child cries incessantly—colic or not—it is normal to have moments where you feel like you are losing control of your own emotions. This was especially true for me when I was alone with my first child. I just kept hanging on to him and hoping it would stop. No one ever told me it was okay to lay down a shrieking baby and move away to collect myself. What a simple and potentially life-saving piece of insight!

Now, years later, I don't know many moms who haven't at some point put their crying child down in a crib, closed the door, and then sat outside the door and cried. Whether he's four months or four years, it's very difficult to hear your child's anguish. It does get easier when you realize his pain—getting a new tooth, scraping a knee, earning a time-out—is not your fault. But when the cries are from a helpless baby, and especially your

"I spent way too much time looking online for answers, doubting my own milk supply and researching alternatives. Finally I had to quit driving myself mad with all the information out there and just accept that it was something he was just going to have to go through and the best I could do was love him through it. I replayed an internal tape in my head telling myself that this was temporary and eventually it would only be a distant memory."

Noell

Ideas for Comforting

- Feed your baby. If you think your baby may be hungry, try a feeding. Hold your baby as upright as possible, and burp your baby often. Sometimes more frequent—but smaller—feedings are helpful. If you're breast-feeding, it may help to empty one breast completely before switching sides. This will give your baby more hindmilk, which is richer and potentially more satisfying than the foremilk present at the beginning of a feeding. Foremilk is the milk, typically lower in fat, available at the beginning of a feeding; hindmilk is milk at the end of a feeding which has a higher fat content than the foremilk. You can even see the darker color and thicker consistency to the milk that is produced at the end of a session, as opposed to the beginning.

- Offer a pacifier. For many babies, sucking is a soothing activity. Even if you're breast-feeding, it's okay to offer a pacifier to help your baby calm down.

- Hold your baby. Cuddling helps some babies. Some will quiet when they're held closely and swaddled in a lightweight blanket. To give your arms a break, try a baby sling, backpack, or other type of baby carrier. Don't worry about spoiling your baby by holding her too much. Spoiled children have learned to use behavior to get what they want. Your newborn is too young to purposefully manipulate you.

- Keep your baby in motion. Gently rock your baby in your arms or in an infant swing. Lay your baby, tummy down, on your knees and then sway your knees slowly. Take a walk with your baby, or buckle your baby in the car seat for a drive. Use a vibrating infant seat or vibrating crib.

Baby

- Sing to your baby. A soft tune might soothe him. And even if lullabies don't stop your baby from crying, they can keep you calm and help pass the time while you're waiting for him to settle down. Playing recorded music may help too.

- Turn up the background noise. Some babies cry less when they hear steady background noise. When holding or rocking your baby, try making a continuous "shhhhh" sound. Turn on a kitchen or bathroom exhaust fan, or play a tape or CD of environmental sounds, such as ocean waves, a waterfall, or gentle rain. Sometimes the tick of a clock or metronome does the trick.

- Use gentle heat or touch. Give your baby a warm bath. Softly massage her, especially around the tummy.

- Look for hidden aggravation. Check for diaper rash. Check for those little plastic strands that connect tags to new clothes. Check your calendar to see if teething could be a factor.

- Give your baby some private time. If nothing else seems to work, a brief time-out might help. Put your baby in his crib for five to ten minutes.

- Consider dietary changes. If you breast-feed, see if eliminating certain foods from your own diet—such as dairy products, citrus fruits, spicy foods, or drinks containing caffeine—has any effect on your baby's crying. If you use a bottle, a new type of bottle or nipple might help.

- Mix it up. Experiment to discover what works best for your baby, even if it changes from day to day.

first, I know what I'm suggesting sounds harsh. But if your arms aren't helping, give them a rest. Put the baby in his crib. Splash water on your face, breathe deeply, and pull yourself together. If you need to, call for help.

Sadly, there's a reason the National Center on Shaken Baby Syndrome exists. When a frustrated caregiver loses control with an inconsolable baby, it takes as little as *five seconds* of shaking to alter that fragile life forever. When you shake a baby, her brain can actually bounce around in her skull. The resulting trauma can mean brain damage, blindness, lifelong disability, or—as in 25 percent of babies with shaken baby syndrome—death.

Think you are too educated or too in control for such an emotional reaction to a crying baby? I hope you never have that theory tested, but it's safer to have a plan of action when you reach your limit. Discuss these realities with your husband and whoever else cares for your child. Tell them what happens when a baby is shaken. Tell them it's fine to call you for help.

Remember that your child's crying is not a reflection of your mommying—your caring attitude is.

Living on Baby Time
My Rattled Daze

1. When my baby cries and I can't comfort her, what do I do?

2. Do I believe it's okay to give myself a time-out and put my baby in a safe place for five to ten minutes when he is crying inconsolably?

3. How is my baby sleeping? Where could I find extra support and good ideas to establish my baby's good sleep habits?

Just One More Thing

Leaving the House

Finding your rhythm at home is challenging enough. Thinking about taking your show on the road can be downright scary. It's a roller coaster you know you need to force yourself to ride. We start looking forward to the wind in our hair and hope to be survivors at the end, but we're pretty darn nervous about what can happen in the middle.

In leaving the house with a baby, one of the most important skills of mothering comes into play: *thinking ahead.* Every day millions of moms do mental gymnastics as they try to anticipate their baby's needs—and it doesn't stop as the child grows. When will she be hungry enough to eat but not so hungry she loses it? What's the best diversion while we wait in line to get the car inspected? How long can we stay at the zoo so she naps at home, not in the car? How can I stuff that piece of gum in my mouth without having to explain why we can't all have one? How long do I realistically have to try on a new pair of jeans with two children in a dressing room the size of a phone booth?

Make no mistake, this anticipating is a skill acquired over time. Don't berate yourself for the goofs you will inevitably make, the moments you'll try to gracefully back out of a situation gone awry. But if you can look at "thinking ahead" as something to learn, like good swaddling or how to spoon-feed a baby without sliming yourself, I think you'll be rewarded. Don't let the anticipation of the what-ifs scare you into staying put. Let them boost your confidence. You need to know how to go and where to go. Notice that "whether to go" is not an option. You need to get out.

That was me one morning. I had made a list of things I needed but could have lived without. If I'd had the courage to write on the list "be around grown-ups," it would have been on the top line. So on this day getting dog food and toothpaste was a great excuse to visit Target.

I had learned not to push my two-month-old's feeding schedule if at all possible, so we stopped in the back of the café area to nurse before shopping. As I sat there happy as can be—feeling composed, feeding this awesome creature, enjoying being out—he pooped. And I mean pooped. The sound was so long and so liquid and gathered so much attention that I started to laugh, until I realized it had exploded out of his diaper, soaked through his onesie, and gotten all over me.

I didn't have extra clothes and really didn't have the stomach to depoop my baby in a public sink. So we were done. I was more amazed than angry at how my morning plans had been derailed. How a person so little could have such a big impact on my time! It was a lesson I learned again and again—that and to always take a fresh baby outfit anywhere you go.

There's a joke among experienced mothers that you can always tell a new mom by how bulging her diaper bag is. In the beginning, you take everything. If that makes you feel more comfortable getting out, then do it. You are not being mocked. We've all been there. Keep in mind that the more you take, the more you have to lose, literally. Shoes for a baby who can't yet roll over, the extra hat, the extra blanket, the six toys "just in case." You increase your odds of losing the diaper bag itself if it's so big you have to continually set it down. If you are running a quick errand, consider just putting a diaper and wipes in your purse and leaving the bag in the car.

I went through three diaper bags before I settled on a rather plain black diaper backpack that has

"I went to Babies R Us more than I needed to simply because there were **people like me** there. I remember my first trip to the mall. I was so proud. I fed her. I changed her. And then she projectile vomited—all the way from the car seat in the stroller to a rack of Liz Claiborne clothes. **Being the responsible mother I was, I ran.**"

Liz

been just awesome. My husband is quite comfortable carrying it, it gives me free arms in an airport, and I'm sure it will still be used when diapers aren't.

Take Ziplocs or plastic grocery bags in whatever diaper bag you use. They are priceless for getting soggy or poopy clothes home or containing a stinky diaper when there's no trash can in sight.

My friend Erika calls her get-ready-to-go area her "launch pad." It consists of a couple rows of hooks at kid-friendly heights, each for a bag prepacked for a given activity. Baby's bag, ballet practice bag, the library bag, and so on. There are hooks designated for coats too. Bags have a home, and they get repacked not in the flurry of an impending departure, but when they are put back on the hook each day.

I hang one of those see-through plastic shoe holders behind my mudroom door, but not for shoes. Everything from sunscreen to mittens to downstairs toothbrushes lives in there to help in getting away from the house without seventeen trips upstairs.

"At the beginning of
parenting,
not being efficient and quick

was a huge
adjustment

for me, one of the toughest.

Now that I'm

used to toddler time,

it'll be hard to see petty things

as time critical when I

go back to work full-time."

Angela

Keep diapers on every level of your home and in hiding places in your car too. In the car, a small, see-through plastic tub for each of your children can help you be prepared with toys, snacks, an extra pacifier, emergency formula, a backup T-shirt, and whatever else the child may need.

Establishing smart habits and your out-and-about rhythm with baby number one will serve you well as your family grows.

My kids used to think it was a game, seeing how many times mommy would run back inside the house for something while everyone was strapped in and ready for takeoff. Once when my parents were in town, we decided to go to the zoo. The car was loaded up with kids, grandparents, and supplies. About the sixth time I got out of the car to get something else, I thought Dad was going to lose it, and my kids no longer found it humorous. It is what it is. I call it colander brain. Inevitably, like slippery strands of spaghetti in a colander, one or two of my thoughts slide out of my brain. And so I go back inside to retrieve that one more thing. I'm getting better, but I've just accepted that no matter how many lists I make, this is the way I am.

For many years I was also known for being late. I used the kids as an excuse, even when they weren't the holdup. I'd joke that I was three weeks late coming out of the womb and had been behind ever since. There's a difference in being on kid time and just being late all the time. It took kindergarten to change my ways. I truly struggled with getting three kids out the door to arrive within the prescribed ten-minute window. But knowing it reflected on my son, I made it work. Not only did I learn to give myself the appropriate amount of time, but I used the time more and more effectively. It mattered, and so I made it happen.

Back in the days of walking the mall with a baby, being on time was the last thing on my mind, even if I was meeting a friend.

"In the workplace you get so much **attention** as a woman who is pregnant with her first baby. And then you are forgotten, and you forget there's a world beyond the walls of your home. So you take your two-week survival diaper bag and you go to the mall. I spent so much time in the Nordstrom lounge. I think William grew up there. I just wanted to be around other women. I didn't know them, but we were **interested** in each other. We were all there because we needed to get out of the house. That lounge saved my life. I was hungry for company."

Susan

Ah, the mall! Where I live, the stroller rodeo starts early under the skylights and around the huge fireplaces of a real shopping beauty. It's a great place to practice getting out with baby. The Nordstrom department store lounge is more like a living room than a ladies' room. Spending time there is a rite of passage for new moms. Women gather to change and nurse babies, bond for three minutes at a time with total strangers, and feel purposeful, as though they are part of a movement. (And I don't mean bowel.)

There's probably a place of similar connection in your area. If you aren't sure, start asking. Maybe it has nothing to do with shopping—but that's highly unlikely. The only downside to a mall is the temptation to spend money. But dozens of women have told me that, besides buying Starbucks coffee or maybe lunch at the food court, they didn't have to spend money to feel great being there, and they became great sale hounds to boot.

When Women
COCOON

Some women are more comfortable staying at home with a new baby. Maybe constant spitting or colicky crying make leaving the house seem too overwhelming. Perhaps nursing in public is too daunting, or you're self-conscious about how you look. One friend told me of staying in because her son hadn't pooped for several days, and she just didn't want to be out when he finally did!

Each mom must proceed at her own pace. And certainly there are days when staying home in your pajamas is highly appealing and downright nurturing. However, if constant tears or feelings of sadness or regret are keeping you inside, consider that you might be experiencing postpartum depression.

The signs include restlessness or irritability; feeling sad, hopeless, and overwhelmed; crying a lot; having no energy or motivation; eating too little or too much; sleeping too little or too much; trouble focusing, remembering, or making decisions; feeling worthless and guilty; a loss of interest or pleasure in activities; withdrawal from friends and family; thoughts of hurting the baby; or a lack of interest in the baby.

If you are experiencing symptoms—which are the result of hormonal shifts and the stresses in your life—talk to your doctor. Postpartum depression is quite treatable with medicine or therapy. It's helpful not to spend a lot of time alone. Open the blinds and let sunlight in. Get dressed and leave the house. Run an errand or take a short walk. Share, share, share.

Millions of women have experienced this fog. It *will* lift.

For more information on postpartum depression, check out another book in this series, *The New Mom's Guide to Your Body after Baby*.

Recently a friend told me she thought the mall appealed to moms because it's a place of guaranteed order when your life is anything but. It's bright and cheery, and other people pick up after you. I also think it's a connection to who we used to be—up on fashion, perhaps with our own income to spend, and surely with a different goal to our wandering. You may not fit as well into other places you used to frequent before baby.

Consider the movies. On the one hand, a sleepy newborn might nurse and nuzzle just fine while you escape into a film. On the other hand, people often go to the movies as a grown-up activity, and a crying infant isn't welcome. Once while out of town, we took our five-month-old to a late movie. He did sleep, eventually, but what I remember is our nervousness as new parents. I've completely forgotten the film.

If you go to a movie and can tolerate some disapproving stares from people expecting the worst when they see you bringing a baby, remember a few things. Consider a late weeknight show when there are lighter crowds. Bring soothing objects for the baby, like a pacifier or a blankie. Time your movie so baby will eat about fifteen minutes into the show. Use lots of hand sanitizer to prevent spreading germs.

Going out to dinner with a baby might seem like a cakewalk after you try a movie! Again, timing is everything. Avoid places with long waits and too much stimulation (blaring music and TVs in every corner) and smoke. Expect to switch off with your dinner partner if baby is awake and needs to be held. To this day it still seems that my husband and I are always eating in shifts—together but in shifts.

The older your baby gets, the more challenging all outings will be as he gets more vocal, more mobile, and more demanding. Get out there with your newborn and sow the seeds of self-confidence. Remember that wherever you go, you can always leave. It's not what happens to you, it's how you

How Do I Love You?
Let Me Count the Places...

Need some good ideas for getting out with baby?

- Meet your husband for lunch.

- Find a MOPS group (MOPS.org) for fellowship with other moms. Child care is provided!

- Try the library. Taking your baby to story time is not ridiculous. It introduces her to a social setting, and it's never too early to read to a child. You can pick up some mental stimulation in the grown-up section at the same time. The same goes for a bookstore. Pick one with a coffee bar!

- Go for a drive to a new place with the windows down and your favorite music up.

- Peruse craft shows, farmers markets, and museums.

- Walk the mall with some other moms.

- When your baby is about six months old, look for swim classes, sign language classes, or mom-and-me exercise classes at the local recreation center.

- Sit in your yard on a blanket with your baby or visit the park—yes, even with a newborn. Enjoy the serendipity of your day—and the temporary immobility of your child. Take the camera and get some sunlit photographs. These days may seem long, but the years fly by.

react to it. You don't get pass or fail marks for outings, just wisdom.

Living on Baby Time
My Rattled Daze

1. What's been my most successful outing? What made it feel that way?

2. What's something I've learned about leaving the house that I'll definitely share with another new mom?

3. What new outing will I try with my newborn? Will I ask someone to go with me or will it just be the baby and me?

Two Jobs to Do

Rhythms of a Working Mom

Kim had just had her first daughter, but back in the office she had no choice but to hit the ground running. A new product was being launched, and she had to fill her seat in the conference room. There wasn't even time to set up her desk.

Sitting in the daylong meeting, her body and the clock told her it was time to pump. "I started to get up," she said. "I was told, 'It is not appropriate for you to leave right now.' So I couldn't get up. I was leaking. I can still remember what I was wearing it was such a vivid moment. Life had changed. I was soaking. This was not how I had envisioned the 'having it all' working mom scenario.

"What I longed for more than anything was some simple empathy, rather than continual stare

"I am a better mom in the long run for my kids when I get away and work. I would be a horrible mommy if I were home all the time without a work identity. I spent fourteen years as a career woman, eight with Universal Studios. It was who I was, and so it was pretty tough to give that up for a while. I love being a mom, but it wasn't my dream from the time I was ten."

Elizabeth

downs as I excused myself from one meeting after another."

Finding your rhythm as a new mom is tough enough. Returning to work adds many new out-of-tune notes to the song your life is trying to sing. All new moms are trying to establish themselves in an overwhelming role. All new moms are making sacrifices. All new moms have a stew of fluctuating hormones and emotions that can slow them down. All new moms have to figure out a way to leave the house with a little person in tow.

For a working mom, all of these challenges must be done in front of co-workers, bosses, and caregivers, not to mention others who judge her decision and expect her former self to show up for work. It's tough, but with organization and a clear sense of your motives, it's doable.

Be honest about the reasons you are staying home or going back to work. Write down the pros and cons and then check them periodically. As

Decisions,
Decisions

Child Care Aware is a national toll-free information line and website for families making child care decisions. There's a great decision-making tool on the website that allows families to organize their thoughts, consider the impact of their decisions, and review the options for finding child care in their area. It's an operation of the National Association of Child Care Resource and Referral Agencies. Check out www .childcareaware.org or call 1-800-424-2246.

you get to know your baby, you will also become better acquainted with the emotional and financial realities of your growing family. Today's decisions might change tomorrow. Go to work but know why you are going. Stay home but be clear on what you are trying to accomplish.

"I write down my motives, my goals. I've tacked them on my bathroom wall and left them in the car. They have to be readily available because I get swayed every single day," my friend Katie relates. "My daughter cut her chin recently, and it was the longest twenty-five-minute ride of my life from work to be with her. I wanted to be the one with the Band-aid. I beat them to the hospital. And there I was again, having to make sure I'm clear on why I'm doing what I'm doing."

In my case, I spent six years trying to have children. In the beginning I assumed day care— a crisp, cute one I had in mind—would become a part of my life. The more I wanted children, the

"Part of it was that I had and have a financial responsibility to my family. Part of it was ego. I was twenty-seven. **Having a child at this stage in my life just wasn't my plan.** I thought I'd just keep moving. It never occurred to me I wouldn't 'keep soldiering on,' as my grandmother would say. I was proud of the fact I was going to carry part of the burden. When I thought about excelling at home, well, I just felt I was worth more than that. When I went back, though, I was immediately conflicted. And I have come to the place that **I love taking care of my family. I truly love it.**"

Kim

more I was in touch with what I wanted to give, not just what I wanted to get from motherhood. I knew this could happen only if I stayed home. But even so, when my son was born, rather than resign from my job, I took a year's leave, after which a job had to be available for me if I wanted it. Maybe I felt an obligation to use my college education. Maybe it was hard to come to terms with how a career can be everything and then become suddenly disposable. Perhaps it was simply easier for my ego to say I was on a leave of absence from a major newspaper than to say I was now "just" a mom. Not that anyone asked. They were too busy smiling at my baby. "Just" a mom—that's laughable when I consider how much work and passion go into a round-the-clock career that changes lives.

Recently I overheard my son tell a friend what I used to do. They spent just six seconds on the topic, but it stopped me in my tracks and unearthed feelings about my identity I thought were pretty well buried. My thoughts on working moms have evolved greatly since my first trip to the delivery room. Yours will too. Let them. And make well-thought-out decisions.

My friend Stacie said she cried the first week of saying good-bye to her son when she left him with the caregiver. Then she and her husband realized tears wouldn't raise a baby, so they became purposeful in maximizing the time they did have together. She couldn't choose not to work, but she could choose her attitude. She was helping her family afford diapers, not French lessons.

"I think if you know you are being the best mother you can be, you can let go of the self-pity or the guilt," she said. "I sang to my baby the entire way home when I picked him up. I didn't waste time."

Elizabeth, who now works part-time from home with kindergarten twins, agreed. "Now I intentionally take that time to go out on the front porch to

What to Look For in Child Care

Reputation. Talk to parents who use the child care center or provider.

Qualified staff. Look for enthusiasm and gentleness. Check on discipline, feeding, and sleeping practices; first aid and CPR training; and staff turnover rates. The American Academy of Pediatrics recommends a 3-to-1 child-staff ratio for babies up to one year old, with a maximum group size of six. The recommended ratio is 4-to-1 for children from twelve to thirty months, with a maximum group size of eight.

Safety. Look for cleanliness in all areas, an emergency plan, and childproofing. Check on the enforcement of sick rules and immunization policies.

Visiting encouraged. You should be able to stop in for a visit unannounced.

A set routine. There should be a schedule, which includes time for rest, play, group and individual activities, snacks, and meals. Ask about the policy for watching TV or videos. Look for the encouragement of creativity and imagination and for age-appropriate toys.

A current license. Check to see if the center is accredited by the National Association for the Education of Young Children. Start with ChildCareAware.org or call 1-800-424-2246.

"I think getting ready to say *good-bye* had to take a backseat to getting ready—period. We tried not to fly around the house, but you just do. I'd always try to take that extra fifteen seconds to pull it together, remind myself of why I had to go to work, and tell myself that my baby was going to be loved on all day. It helped."

Kristi

look at the roly-poly or other fascinating bugs. That ten-minute investment is everything. You choose to read the book at night. You don't turn on the TV."

To help Katie focus exclusively on her kids in the evenings, she organizes everything else she can in advance. She opens mail daily and near the trash can to avoid a pileup. Grocery shopping happens only once a week. Laundry waits till the weekend. Meals are planned. And two nights a month are reserved for mom, when she can do something she enjoys by herself.

Mornings can be pretty hairy for working parents who have had a particularly hard night with the baby or find spit-up on their dry-clean-only clothes on the way out the door. Trying to fold a load of laundry or pay a couple of bills when you should be getting out the door will only add to your stress. Stay focused on a calm transition. Learn to leave some things undone.

My friend Stephanie remembers life with her first baby: "I did it wrong for a while. I could not get to work on time. I followed Ashley's schedule until I realized I had to set the pace. I had to decide when we started our day."

Stacie's husband, Tim, would drop their son at a cousin's, who then took him to Tim's mom's home for the day. Stacie had a forty-five-minute commute in a different direction, and so they repeated the two-leg process in the evening. Another friend handed her baby girl to a relative at a gas station, as her commute and her relative's home dictated. It's a tough memory for her.

Even if you are fortunate enough to leave baby at home with a caregiver, planning ahead emotionally and logistically will help you get in a groove and be better prepared when that last-minute diaper blowout happens.

Elizabeth recalled being ready to leave for work one morning when one of her twins had a leaky

"I couldn't speak my mind about how she *cared* for my child. And it took away from her being just Grandma because eventually she had to be a disciplinarian. I would feel guilty for not checking in every three hours."

Stephanie

poop, so she changed her and her clothes, and then her brother's, since they wore matching outfits. Then he threw up. "Not necessary," she said in hindsight. "You learn."

Deciding who cares for your child while you work is a highly personal decision that takes time. Consider the takeaways on pages 115 and 117 from two moms who chose their mother-in-law to care for their new baby.

You can ask every working mom you know what she's done and you still might not hear what's right for *your* family. The good news is if something doesn't work, you can adjust. One friend I know went through four caregivers for her twins before she found the one who has been with the family for five years. Katie went through seven child care situations. Her best advice: be secure in your role as a mom while also being comfortable with someone else loving your children.

"He got the most *love* he possibly could have outside of me.

That alone mattered more than the stuff we did differently."

Stacie

At work, mothers quickly learn that they don't shed one hat to wear another. The hats just pile up. If you wait tables, you look at families in a different light. If you teach, your empathy for children—and their parents—expands. Whatever you sell, whomever you serve, you now add to your job the perspective of a woman with a child. It's a beautiful thing to have mothers in the workplace. You can relate more fully to co-workers with children too.

Hopefully your work environment and supervisor can adjust to your new role. Tardiness is inevitable once in a while, as are unexpected sick days or leaving at midday to pick up a child who has a fever. The really fun adjustment for those with male bosses is taking breaks to pump milk.

"I had a boss who was appalled I would have to retreat three times a day to pump," my friend Stephanie remembers. "I had a dream job, and this

"We finally got off the formal daycare path and went to find a grandma. We wanted our kids to feel like family never left. And we wanted warm meals and hugs and kisses over major early childhood development. It's different for everyone, but just figuring that out was a blessing to us. My mistake was thinking my influence couldn't be felt until I was home. I thought my nanny was the expert. I wished she would call me at work. I wished I'd said, 'Please talk a lot about mommy and daddy.' I never asked her to. As a new mom, you lack confidence and think, *Everybody knows my child better than me.* I didn't trust my instincts and lean on God enough. It was a tough time that existed quietly in my soul for a long time."

Kim

Making It Work

Plan for the morning the night before. Choose clothes for both you and baby. Have your bag and/or breast pump packed or even in the car. Set out breakfast. Taking care of the "stuff" in advance will leave you more energy for the emotion of the morning and the unexpected happenings.

Get up early. Getting yourself ready first frees you to focus on baby's needs and bonding with him. Consider playing soft music instead of the morning news to set a peaceful tone.

Have an honest conversation with your boss in advance of returning to work. Discuss any changes to your routine you may have to make to accommodate pumping, daycare hours, and any other responsibilities. Don't use this conversation for an emotional dump. Stick to the facts.

If using an individual caregiver, spend time together before your first day of work. Have her over for lunch. Talk about what happens when she or baby is sick, how often you plan to check in, and what happens when she runs late or you do. You can't anticipate everything that might come up, but establishing an honest rapport can save you angst later on.

Remember that you and your husband are partners. Make your marital relationship a priority—even if it means staying up late to check in with one another. Share your feelings on being a working mom. Listen to his feelings on leaving the baby with a caregiver as well. And then share things that have nothing to do with work or baby!

Discuss household duties with your spouse. Decide together who will do what and the things you can let go, as you find your new routine.

Cultivate a support system of moms who have been where you are. Some MOPS groups (MOPS.org) meet in the evening. At these meetings you can ask other moms what worked for them and what didn't.

was a whole new challenge I had to face. The flow of your day, your time, it's not your own, whether you're at home or work."

Before you return to work, talk to your supervisor about your need to pump milk. Especially if that boss is male, be straightforward but not graphic. He might have a wife or sister and be familiar with your situation, or it may throw him for a loop.

Determine where you can do it, how long your breaks can be and how frequent, and where you can store the milk. You'll need enough storage containers to make it through the day and a cooler for transporting milk home safely. It's always a good idea to have an extra shirt at work in case your breasts leak, as well as a small blanket for privacy and a do-not-disturb sign for the door. One of my workplaces hung a big "Got Milk?" poster on the door of a room deemed the "lactation lounge" because of a number of

Home Work
Reaping the Benefits while Getting Something Done

Welcoming baby to a home that's also a home office brings its own challenges. Whether it's you or your husband—or both—who manage a career from home, the key to a productive rhythm is setting up a space and a routine that lets you enjoy the perks of being together.

Just because you are at home doesn't mean you can work and parent *at the same time*. Especially as your baby grows, you'll need to consider in-home caregiving, even if you're there.

Here are some things to consider:

- Use a headset with a quickly accessible mute button.
- Schedule important calls during nap time or a designated time when baby is out with someone else on errands or play dates.
- Plan lunch together as a family.
- Be honest with your clients or customers to diffuse the stress of always feeling you need silence when you are on the phone. There's no reason to hide that you're in a home office, as millions are these days.
- Use earplugs if you need to.

- Close the door when you need to.
- Be respectful of the job being done and don't poke your head in on a whim and break your spouse's concentration.
- Save those old keyboards! Soon enough your baby will be pounding away with you.
- When you're off, be off. Setting limits on your work hours is even more important when you have little ones to love.
- Be realistic. Where you live, the size of your family, or the nature of your job may make a home office unworkable.

new moms in the office. You may not want to be that on display, but it certainly normalized for the rest of the office a routine happening in the lives of several women.

As in all things maternal, your attitude makes a big difference in pumping at work. Being relaxed encourages the letdown reflex and will get you back to your desk quicker. Looking at a picture of your baby helps too. If you make pumping as normal and personal as brushing your teeth, then it will be. If you make a big deal of toting milk around or being "ready to burst" or misuse your pumping breaks, the attention you get may not be positive.

Remember, all mothers continually reassess what they are doing, why they are doing it, and how they can best parent their children. If you have children and are working outside the home, you have two careers. This makes it all the more important that you find your rhythm.

Living on Baby Time
My Rattled Daze

1. I work because . . .

   I don't work because . . .

2. Does my husband support my working outside of the home? Have we discussed how we will divide up the household responsibilities so that my working is realistic?

3. When and how will I reassess how staying at home or being a working parent is going? What does a successful rhythm look like for my family?

Permission Granted

Time for Mom

Being a new mom is at once exhilarating and stifling. Knowing someone is fully dependent on you is one thing, but now you are dependent on someone else too—if you want to go anywhere without your child. This is definitely not baby shower conversation.

It first hit me when my son was five months old and I needed an emergency root canal. I was hurting so bad and still I had to make the calls and impose on someone else so I could have the pleasure of having my tooth drilled. While I was grateful for my sister's willingness and ability to take a half day off work—my husband was out of town—I remember feeling pretty humbled by my limits, and more than a little ornery too.

Over time I think moms learn to work with the reality of needing child care and needing time for themselves. You get creative. You appreciate a fifteen-minute errand you get to do alone. And if you're like me, you take showers that are too long and too hot, soaking in the solitude and steaming away the world.

When my friend Angela's first son was a baby, as soon as her husband got home, she'd often take off for Starbucks for an hour. She'd sit, drink coffee, and read a newspaper. I'm not sure if I was jealous or judgmental, but I wondered why she had to leave her home. When I had my third child, I finally understood. Coincidentally, that's also when I started drinking coffee!

"You ask yourself, *Is he safe?* Then you do what you need to do. We can't be replaced as mothers, but it's okay to leave and to want to leave. You need to be rejuvenated," Angela says.

"If you have a bad week at work you can say, 'Friday's coming.' When you are a new mom, there is no weekend. It doesn't stop. So I started to grab my weekend throughout the week. Fifteen minutes at a time to do something for me. One nap at a time. If I couldn't get a real break, I tried to find the mental time away."

Noell

Angela also dealt with the monotony of care giving by approaching it as she approached her careers—trying to be the best she could. She'd research and read on child development, she became a trained presenter of the Love and Logic parenting/teaching method, and she was always looking for experiences to enhance motherhood and childhood for her boys. She looked to vary her rhythm, as that made life—just like music—much more enjoyable.

The more children you have, the more assertive you have to be about getting time to nurture yourself—or just get that badly needed haircut. I've thought about going to my husband with a permission slip to sign, to highlight how it feels as though I have to get permission to do something—anything—alone. But I think he gets it. Once I took nine months to use a spa gift certificate he gave me one Mother's Day. He *gave* it to me, and still I felt guilty going off to use it. I wish I'd started earlier making regular time for me because it does get easier when you realize how revitalizing it is.

Women have to be judicious about choosing their escapes. There is much daytime television out there that isn't healthy for your brain or your body—not talking "Oprah" here—but it's a quick fix when you're stuck in the house and want to "go" somewhere else. We all love a *People* magazine once in a while, but motherhood is for the long haul. Losing yourself in soap operas or celebrity news doesn't nourish your soul. Neither does food or alcohol or shopping.

As you think about getting "permission" to take care of yourself, I want to also give you permission to have mixed feelings about this new world order.

Parenting is hard the first time. You make mistakes. You drown in ignorance. You wonder how the women on the darn commercials have bright complexions and spotless floors for their babies to crawl on. And you might wonder if this is what you

"I kept thinking, *If I can just get through this time nursing.* I would pray for the sun to come up again and hope I could do another day. **I lost myself.** I grew up watching *Little House on the Prairie*. Caroline Ingalls—that was going to be me. Baking, being all calm and loving and welcoming dad home with a hug, family life being everything and my kids loving me. **I didn't count on being so tired I couldn't remember if I fed the baby.** It was hard to find glory, or validation, in what I was doing. But it happened. I started to find purpose and joy in my family."

Noell

signed up for. Maybe you are waiting to feel the warm fuzzies of being a mom that you expected would come automatically.

Vanessa struggled with the lack of an immediate connection to her second son—even more surprising to her because he was indeed her second. She attributes the delay to the five days he fought jaundice, under special lights so that she couldn't even cuddle him after a feeding. Add that to a miscarriage between children, and Vanessa realized this baby started life as more of a medical project than a person.

This is the case for many new moms who have suffered infertility before having a baby. They are used to healing from—or distancing themselves altogether from—another negative pregnancy test. There's support and attention when you are struggling to achieve and maintain a pregnancy, but when you are a new mom, you are on your own, considered "normal" all of a sudden.

You have to share your feelings, wherever they originated and whatever they are. Don't add to your stress or disappointment by stuffing them down deep and hoping they'll disappear. My experience is that just speaking an issue out loud can help lessen its intensity in your heart.

"It's okay to say to your friends and family, 'I'm not enjoying myself right now.' I totally thought I couldn't complain because I was home," one friend said. "This is what I wanted. But in the beginning you think it's going to be more satisfying. I had to talk that out."

Give it a few months. When your baby is six weeks old, make an effort to get in a rhythm, a routine. Reach out to connect with other moms, and keep watching that baby. Seeing those smiles—the early ones you know are meant only for you— will change your relationship to your child and to your job as a mom. Suddenly you realize you

"People knew we had struggled with infertility; they knew how much we wanted this child. To assure that the whole experience was perfect, I felt like I needed to love everything. I bargained with God and said, 'Give me a baby, and I'll be the *perfect* mom.' I had it in my head how it should be. I wasn't prepared for the imperfections. My life had been on schedule. I'd always looked for the next goal. Now I didn't know what the goal was."

Liz

aren't alone. There's a little buddy ready to blossom inside those footed jammies.

When my oldest was six months old, I attended one of my first MOPS meetings. It was fall, the leaves were changing, and sitting with other mothers twice a month was changing my perspective on what it meant to be home with a child. After losing two pregnancies, I already knew motherhood was a calling, a privilege. But now I was *seeing* it, by sharing the fun and frustration of the journey with other women.

On the way home from that meeting, though my son was pretty tired after only a brief nap in MOPS child care, something inspired me to take a spontaneous left turn. There was a park I'd been told had awesome fall foliage. I happened to have my camera.

My baby boy adored exploring the crunchy gold carpet I'd set him on. His plaid hat framed a beautiful toothless grin. As I clicked the camera, I started to cry. I knew that every infertility treatment and grieving hour and labor push and sleepless night had been worth it. I needed no permission to be here. I was the mom.

Living on Baby Time
My Rattled Daze

1. What has surprised me most about becoming a mom?

2. Where would I go and what would I do if I had four hours by myself?

3. Have I given myself permission to get away from my baby? How have I handled the need for child care?

9

Daddy Dish

Living in Different
Daytime Worlds

Whadya do today, honey?"

"Well, I put clothes on. Put clothes on the baby. Put more clothes on the baby after she pooped out of that pink thing I like so much. I called my mom but got off the phone because the baby wasn't latching on real well . . .

"I went to the store but got only some of the things on my list because I realized I was leaking and didn't time our outing very well. I unloaded the dishwasher halfway and opened some of the mail. We played patty-cake—I really think she smiled! I made her next doctor's appointment, but I think I might change it since your mom is coming in town. I put those shirts in the car but didn't quite get them to the dry cleaners. You know, the store debacle . . .

"I had plans for making this new thing for dinner, but since I didn't get all the stuff, I decided we'd have burgers instead . . . Ooooh. Forgot to thaw out the meat. Feel like a pizza?"

"So you didn't really do *anything*?"

Hand this book to your husband right now.

Husbands, try never to come home and ask "*What* did you do today?" Chances are, the laundry list of attempts will make you dizzy. Your response, though well-intentioned and even factual, could put your wife over the edge. The better question is "*How* was your day, dear?" That way, if she didn't *do* a darn thing to completion, she doesn't have to be reminded. Okay, hand the book back.

When you are intently looking for your new rhythm as a mom, it's easy to forget things have changed quite a bit for dad too. He's operating as his former self at work on his current sleep budget, which is likely tight. He's trying to navigate your fluctuating sense of purpose, mom-confidence, and sleep deficit. And he's also trying to use the limited hours he has at home to establish himself as daddy in the eyes of the newest member of your household.

Even though he probably leaves every day for work, it's a new rhythm for him too. Maybe you're thinking, *No way. Nothing has changed for him, and my life is upside down.* Ask him. Gently. But don't do it during the workday.

I'm extremely guilty of picking up the phone during the day when I have a thought I desperately want to share. He's my best friend and daddy to my crazy crew—of course it's him I want to call. But he's also employed, with co-workers usually within earshot of his cell phone. So I'm trying to be more judicious.

We've developed an understanding that if I call and he can't talk, he simply says, "Call ya back," and hangs up without waiting for me to respond. When I was alone with baby, wanting to share something he did—something monumental I'm sure, like toot—I didn't take well to being cut short. But of course that was selfish. And now I'm the one who often cuts him short during a daytime call as chaos reigns around me or I don't have an extra thirty seconds before needing to get someone somewhere. I'm so grateful for the times my husband has let me ramble, as when our middle son emptied a bag of flour on top of his head, and I just had to describe the scene in great detail.

Ask your husband about the rhythm of his day, when it's best to touch base, and when it's not a good time. You may think you know but you're probably experiencing more things than ever that you want to share, and that might cloud your judgment as you reach for the phone.

Some of my friends practice "couch time." For fifteen minutes after husband gets home, they sit and recap the day, with a rule of no interruptions. Both get heard, but the idea here is deeper: mom and dad's relationship is sacred, and this is sacred time. Three increasingly vocal sons, who adore attacking their dad as soon as he arrives, make this tough for us. Perhaps if we'd begun doing it with one sleeping newborn, it wouldn't be so hard now. It's crucial for your kids to see you giving your marriage top priority.

During the day, I've been known to actually keep a list of what I want to tell my husband. It prevents verbal diarrhea on my part when he walks in the door, and I can wait until it's quiet enough to share because I'm not worried about something slipping out of my head. When Todd is out of town, our kids keep a daddy box that gets filled with treasures, school papers, and assorted things we want to share. And when he gets back, it's great fun to roll it out. This comes in handy, especially when we are in different time zones and phone time is tough. Sometimes I put my own thoughts in there with the kids' stuff.

However you do it, the point is to respect each other's evolving rhythms and keep on communicating.

Living on Baby Time
My Rattled Daze

1. What time of day are my husband and I most likely to have a productive conversation? When are we least likely to communicate effectively?

2. How can I better communicate my feelings and my needs to my husband?

3. How can I encourage a good relationship between my husband and our child?

4. How can I let my husband know that even when I'm busy with the baby, our relationship is my top priority?

Making
Sweet Music

The Changing Melodies
of Motherhood

D rums." For years on my self-indulgent Christmas lists, that's what this little girl wrote. Odd for a girl, odder perhaps for a girlie girl like me. But there was something I loved about the way two hands could work separately and yet together. A song could start with a single beat, and then the song could swallow the beat, but it was still there underneath, giving life to the music. Who doesn't love drummers? They are the mysterious men in the background, at least usually men anyway, but you can always look forward to their moment in the spotlight, because there's never a wasted second. What energy! I always thought. What coordination!

I never got those drums—and no apologies necessary, Mom and Dad. I understand why. But these days I might as well be a drummer, the energetic, hopefully coordinated, multitasking, behind-the-scenes drummer in this band we call a family. My quest is to create a rhythm that drives us forward. It may be even sometimes, unsteady at others, but it's ours.

You'll find your rhythm as a mom. The music may seem chaotic right now. It is. And just when you think you hear sweet stability, the song will change. You'll have to adjust what you do and when and how. Raising children is a series of new songs, and you are a composition in the works too. Just remember, you're not on stage alone. Love your band and keep on drumming. Here's to making the music that's right for you.

Acknowledgments

From Susan

Thank you to the dozens of women who shared with me their ups and downs, moments of great triumph and great disgust, and the yearning and yelling in their hearts. You elevate the calling of motherhood by your intense love, dedication, and authenticity.

MOPS has enhanced mothering around the world and now across generations. I am confident, and deeply grateful, that its ripple effects will be felt throughout my family tree. Beth Lagerborg, thank you for asking me to dwell with you, in God's perfect timing.

Thank you to Dr. Monica Reed for reviewing this project for medical relevance and accuracy and for her dedication to women's health.

This book was possible because of women I love and was written for women I don't know, including the ones who will one day love my boys. Zach, Luke, and A.J., you are life's most amazing gifts and most humbling projects. Todd, your love inspires me. Our journey with them and with God is transforming my heart. Thank you for never giving up on my becoming a mom.

From Monica

I would like to acknowledge the team at MOPS International—Mary Beth Lagerborg, Carla Foote, and Jean Blackmer—who extended the opportunity to me to be involved in this wonderful "labor" of love; Lee Hough with Alive Communications—who continues to be an ardent supporter; and last but not least my husband, my children, and my God—all of whom make my life a wonder-filled adventure.

Susan Besze Wallace was a newspaper reporter for twelve years coast to coast, most recently with the *Denver Post*, before leaving to focus on the daily deadlines of sons Zach, Luke, and A.J. She led one of the largest MOPS (Mothers of Preschoolers) groups in the country and is a contributor to *MOMSense* magazine. Susan and husband Todd recently transplanted their busy brood to northern Virginia, where she continues writing freelance news stories and celebrating the roller coaster of motherhood in print.

Dr. Monica Reed is a physician, author, and speaker and has dedicated her life to promoting health, healing, and wellness. She currently serves as CEO of Florida Hospital Celebration Health. Dr. Reed is the author of *Creation Health Breakthrough: 8 Essentials to Revolutionize Your Health Physically, Mentally and Spiritually*. She and her husband Stanton Reed have two daughters: Melanie and Megan.

Better together…

MOPS is here to come alongside you
during this season of early mothering to
give you the support and resources you
need to be a great mom.

Get connected today!

Mothers of Preschoolers

2370 S. Trenton Way, Denver CO 80231
888.910.MOPS • **www.MOPS.org/bettermoms**

Perfect Gifts for a New Mom!

New moms run into a host of new challenges once baby arrives. *The New Mom's Guides* go straight to the heart of these matters, offering moms guidance and encouragement in this new season of life.